T0060285

The Mandala COLORING BOOK

VOLUME II

Relax, Calm Your Mind, and Find Peace with 100 Mandala Coloring Pages

JIM GOGARTY

Founder of iHeartMandalas.com

Adams Media

New York London Toronto Sydney New Delhi

Copyright © 2016 by Jim Gogarty.
All rights reserved.
This book, or parts thereof, may not be reproduced in any form without
permission from the publisher; exceptions are made for brief excerpts used in
published reviews.

Published by
Adams Media
An Imprint of Simon & Schuster, Inc.
100 Technology Center Drive
Stoughton, MA 02072

ISBN 10: 1-4405-9593-3
ISBN 13: 978-1-4405-9593-6

Printed in the United States of America.

5 2022

This book is intended as general information only, and should not be used to
diagnose or treat any health condition. In light of the complex, individual, and
specific nature of health problems, this book is not intended to replace professional
medical advice. The ideas, procedures, and suggestions in this book are intended
to supplement, not replace, the advice of a trained medical professional. Consult
your physician before adopting any of the suggestions in this book, as well as
about any condition that may require diagnosis or medical attention. The author
and publisher disclaim any liability arising directly or indirectly from the use of
this book.

Many of the designations used by manufacturers and sellers to distinguish their
products are claimed as trademarks. Where those designations appear in this book
and Simon & Schuster, Inc. was aware of a trademark claim, the designations
have been printed with initial capital letters.

Cover design by Sylvia McArdle and Nicola DosSantos.
Cover and interior images © Jim Gogarty.

INTRODUCTION

Mandalas are the perfect entry point for meditation. The word *mandala* is loosely translated from ancient Indian Sanskrit to mean "circle," and these particular circles are powerful symbols that have been used by different cultures for thousands of years to represent balance, the circle of life, and a sense of unity and connection with all things. Buddhists have been using the mandala to help them clear their minds, focus, and pave the way for meditation for centuries, and now with *The Mandala Coloring Book, Volume II*, you can do the same.

The simple act of coloring in the 100 mandalas found throughout this book will help you "enter the mandala" and reap some real therapeutic and physical benefits, including:

* Relaxation
* A sense of well-being
* Increased focus
* Increased creativity
* Reduced blood pressure
* Reduced stress and anxiety

How does this work? Coloring forces your mind to focus on the task at hand—filling in the mandala—which doesn't leave room for it to focus on stress, worry, and fear. The reduction of these negative thoughts creates a sense of balance that's strengthened by the inherent meditative quality of the mandala. After spending just a short time coloring and letting your meditative mind wander, you find yourself living a life that's happier, healthier, and more in tune with the world around you. A clear mind and a healthy body are just a meditation away, so pick up your pencil and set your mind free.

HOW TO USE THIS BOOK

Begin the meditation process by choosing the materials you'll use to do your coloring. Some people prefer pencils, some prefer crayons, and others prefer felt-tip pens or even paints. When considering this, think about whether you would like to blend and shade your colors like you can do with pencils or whether you prefer the bright, solid colors you can achieve with felt-tip pens. Any option is okay; just choose one that feels right to you.

Next, browse your way through the book and stop when you come across a mandala that feels right. Your subconscious mind knows what it needs and the mandala you pick will be the meditative tool that's right for the moment. Keep in mind that some mandalas can be colored relatively quickly while others are more complex and will require a bit more time. Think about how much time you have available. Do you want to finish the coloring in one session? Are you happy to complete it over time?

Once you have your materials ready and you've chosen your mandala, you're ready to start coloring. But how should you begin? Choosing your colors is a very personal thing and no one can tell you what colors should be used for any specific mandala. If you want to lay your crayons or colored pencils out in front of you and pick them up at random, that's okay. Your mandala will be colored in the way it's supposed to be. If you want to plan out the colors you'll use based on your mood or preferences, that's fine too. Keep in mind that various colors can represent various things, for example:

* White = purity, innocence, positivity
* Red = passion, strength, power, danger
* Orange = enthusiasm, happiness, creativity
* Yellow = energy, intelligence, joy
* Green = growth, harmony, fertility
* Blue = loyalty, wisdom, truth
* Violet = nobility, wealth, ambition
* Black = evil, death, mystery

Of course, sometimes a color is just a color, but looking at the symbolism of the colors you choose can help you gain access into your subconscious mind.

Whether you begin to color your mandala from the outside or inside can also give you insight into your mind and meditation. It has been suggested that when you begin coloring the mandala at the outside edge and make your way inward toward the center, you explore your inner self. Conversely, working from the center of the mandala outward can help you feel more connected to the universe around you. In addition, it's common to color the mandala in a symmetrical fashion, representing order and balance. This can be through straightforward mirror symmetry or complex radial symmetry, working from the center outward in radial-type fashion.

Each mandala will be unique to you in color and design so take a deep breath, set your cares aside, and start coloring.

ABOUT THE AUTHOR

JIM GOGARTY has had a passion for drawing for as long as he can remember, going from crayons to felt tips to today's digital pen. He began drawing mandalas in 2005 after a spiritual awakening during meditation. Since then, he has worked to turn this love for the symmetrical patterns into a career. He currently runs iHeartMandalas.com, where he brings these images to life. He currently lives in Hertfordshire, England with his supportive partner Susan and two children, Lillith and Charlie.